Aesop's Fables

Happy House

About Wise & Wide

- A systematic 6-level English reading program based on Lexile® measures
- Diverse and interesting topics chosen from the elementary curriculums of Korea and English speaking western countries
- Well-written books in various forms including fiction stories, descriptive texts, and classics retold
- The informative but original fiction stories grab your interest, leading to the easy and clear understanding of the educational content.
- Improve thinking skills with solid after-reading activities at all levels of the series.

Wise & Wide is a 6-level English reading program that consists of 60 books and each level is systematically divided by Lexile® measures. The Lexile® Framework for Reading is the most popular reading measuring system in American formal education curriculums and many English programs. Over 20 out of 50 states in the U.S. mark Lexile® measures directly on students' final report cards and over 300 well-known publishers adopt and use Lexile® measures.

Experience many kinds of readings written by professional writers from the U.S. and England. They used interesting topics that were carefully chosen after analyzing elementary curriculums from around the world including Korea, the U.S., England, and Australia among many others. Comprehensive after-reading activities including graphic organizers, speaking tasks, and After-reading Tests are ready for you.

Levels in the series and their corresponding Lexile® measures

Level	Lexile® measures	U.S. Grade
Level 1	Below 200L	Pre K - K
Level 2	190L - 400L	Lower Grade 1
Level 3	350L - 530L	Upper Grade 1
Level 4	420L - 650L	Grade 2
Level 5	520L - 940L	Grade 3 - 4
Level 6	830L - 1070L	Grade 5 - 6

＊ Smart Readers: Wise & Wide level 1 is applicable to the preschool level in the U.S.
＊ The source of the relationship between Lexile® measures and U.S. school grades: CCSS(Common Core State Standards) FOR ENGLISH LANGUAGE ARTS, APPENDIX A (2012, which is used by 45 states in the U.S.)

Topic List

	Level 1	Level 2	Level 3	Level 4	Level 5	Level 6
Book 1	Science>Biology: The hibernation of animals Story	Science>Biology: Living and nonliving things Story	Science>Biology> Animals & the Environment: Sea otters Story	Environment> Living with nature: The diver & the persimmon tree Story	Science>Biology> Animal: Amazing animals of the Amazon Story	Science>Biology: Germs, transmitted diseases Story
Book 2	Literature> World classics: Aesop's fables Story	Literature> Traditional fairy tale: Old tales about stones Story	Social Studies> Economy: To run a business to make and save money Story	Science>Biology> Plants: Photosynthesis Story	Science>Earth science: Earth's layers, earthquakes, volcanoes, and earth's atmosphere Report	Mathematics> Sequence: The golden ratio & the Fibonacci sequence Story
Book 3	Science>Physics: How shadows are formed Story	Literature> World classics: Peter Pan Story	Science>Scientific technology: Nanobots Story	Literature>Myths: World's creation stories Story	Literature> Legend: The story of King Arthur Story	Literature>Myths: Constellation myths Story
Book 4	Literature> Traditional literature: The Talmud Story	Science>Biology> Animal: Polar bears Story	Science>Biology> Animal: Mountain gorillas Story	Social Studies> Cultural anthropology: Amazing ancient cultures of the world Story	Science> Earth science: Clouds and weather Story	Literature> Human & animals: The friendship between a girl and a horse Story
Book 5	Social Studies> Ethics: Rules in daily life Story	Science>Biology: The five senses Report	Social Studies> Cultural anthropology: Astonishing festivals Report	Art>Music: Stories from two operas Story	Social Studies> World culture & history: The Renaissance Story	Sports> Board sports: Surfing & snowboarding Story
Book 6	Social Studies> World geography & travel: Tourist attractions around the world Story	Science>Biology> Animal: Dinosaurs Story	Science> Astronomy: The solar system Story	Social Studies> People: Three great people who overcame hardships Story	Science>Scientific technology: The wonderful world of robots Report	Art>Music: Composers of the Romantic Era Report
Book 7	Science> Space science: The life of astronauts Report	Social Studies> Cultural anthropology: Mythological monsters from around the world Report	Mathematics> Elementary mathematics: Numbers, measurement, shapes and data Report	Science & Social Studies> Technology & culture: Inventions from around the world Report	Art>Works of art: Famous paintings Report	Social Studies> Human & animals: Animals in action for human Report
Book 8	Social Studies> Cultural anthropology: Various living cultures of the world Story	Art>Music: Instruments in the orchestra Story	Social Studies> Life safety: Learning and using outdoor survival skills Story	Social Studies> History: The California Gold Rush Report	Social Studies & Science> Psychology: Psychology in everyday life Story	Literature> World classics: The Merchant of Venice Story
Book 9	Social Studies> Jobs: Interviews about jobs Report	Science>Scientific technology: Developments in technology in different times Story	Social Studies> Politics>Election: Running for 3rd grade class president Story	Literature> World classics: Stories of Sherlock Holmes Story	Literature> World classics: Adrift in the Pacific Story	Social Studies> History & People: Great world leaders in history Report
Book 10	Literature>Traditional fairy tale: Eastern and Western folk tales on the same theme Story	Sports>Winter sports: Various aspects of some Winter Olympic sports Report	Literature> World classics: Short stories by O. Henry Story	Sports> Ball games: Various aspects of popular ball games Report	Social Studies> History: Famous events that changed world history Report	Art & Social Studies> Art: Stories about the creation, distribution, and preservation of paintings Report

How to Use This Book

•Before Reading

You can easily find the topic and what kind of story you are about to read.

•The text

All the stories were written by professional writers from the U.S. and England, so you will read authentic and appropriate English sentences and expressions in every book in the series.

•Pop Quiz

Check out right away if you understand what you have just read by solving a pop quiz that checks your comprehension.

•Key Words

The key words and expressions on each page are listed for you to easily study them.

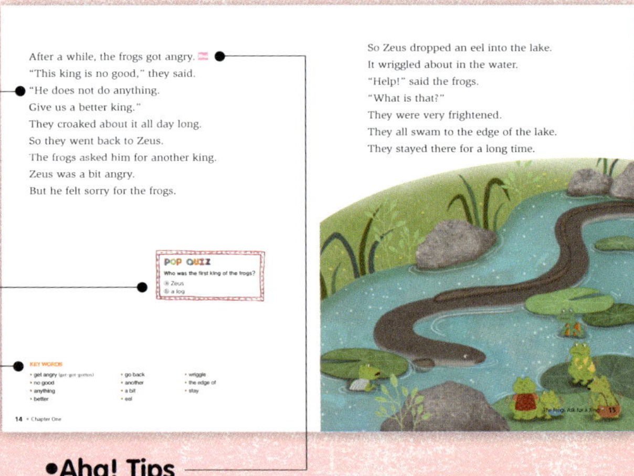

•Aha! Tips

Download free Korean explanations at *www.ihappyhouse.co.kr* for all of the sentences marked with "Aha!". These explain cultural, scientific, and economic knowledge or they deal with aspects of English such as grammatical structures or idiomatic expressions. There are lots of "Aha! Tips" to help you understand the text.

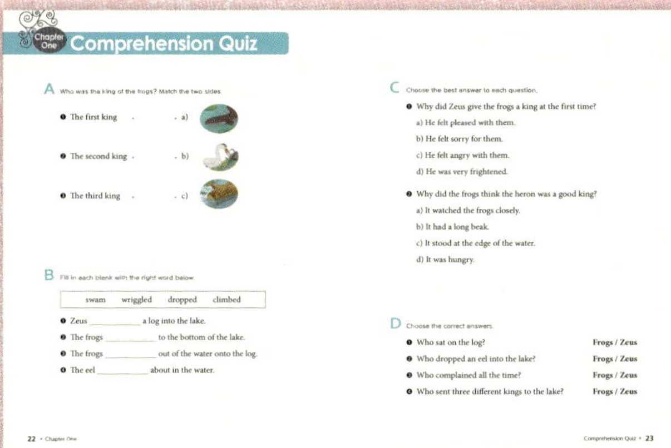

•Comprehension Quiz

After reading one chapter, solve various questions to find out if you fully understand the content.

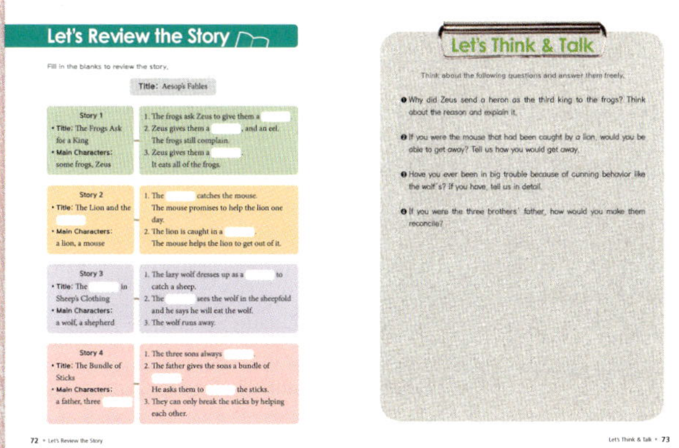

•Let's Review the Story / •Let's Think & Talk

Fill in the blanks in the organizer to summarize the whole story. Express your own thinking and feelings about the story by answering the questions. You can build up logic and reasoning skills for your essay examinations in the future.

Appendix

Audio Files

The texts are read vividly by American professional voice actors.

(Audio files downloaded for free)

After-reading Test

Solve an additionally provided After-reading Test for each book.

The Korean translation, Answer Keys, a Word Quiz, a Word List, and Aha! Tips for each book

You can download them for free at *www.ihappyhouse.co.kr* or *www.darakwon.co.kr*

Before Reading

Aesop's Fables

Level 1–2,
Lexile® 190L

•Literature〉World Classics
•Story

Developing wisdom with Aesop's Fables!

Living in ancient Greece, Aesop wrote a collection of fables. According to records, Aesop used to be a slave, but he was such a great story-teller that he was given his freedom.

The fables are usually short stories. The main characters in the stories are not only humans, but also animals and plants which are given human qualities. The fables explain various aspects of human behavior and try to teach us a lesson. Well-known stories such as 'The Boy Who Cried Wolf,' 'The Fox and the Grapes,' 'Belling the Cat,' 'The Goose That Laid the Golden Eggs' are good examples of *Aesop's Fables*.

Think about what wisdom of life each fable wants to give us when you read the four stories included in the book.

The Frogs Ask for a King

Frogs that ask Zeus for a king! But no matter what kind of king is sent, they aren't satisfied. What should Zeus do to deal with the displeased frogs?

The Lion and the Mouse

There is a Korean saying 'Even when you are taken away by a tiger, you can survive if you calm yourself down'. Here is a mouse that escaped from a lion without being eaten. How did the mouse survive?

The Wolf in Sheep's Clothing

A wolf looking at a flock of sheep and figuring out how to prey on them! Can the wolf prey on the sheep?

The Bundle of Sticks

Three brothers who never listen and always argue with each other! How can their father make these three hopeless brothers reconcile?

Contents

Aesop's Fables

Aesop's Fables

The Frogs Ask for a King

Many frogs lived in a lake.

It was a huge lake.

The frogs swam around.

They ate flies.

But they could not agree on who was in charge.

"We need a king," they said.

They croaked about it all day long.

So they went to the god Zeus. **Aha!**

They asked him for a king.

▲ Zeus

KEY WORDS

- ask for
- live in
- lake
- huge
- **swim around** (swim-swam-swum)
- **eat** (eat-ate-eaten)
- fly
- agree on

- be in charge
- need
- croak
- about
- all day long
- so
- god

Zeus felt sorry for the frogs.

"I will give them a king," he said.

He dropped a log into the lake.

It went *SPLASH* into the
water.

"Help!" cried the
frogs.

"What is that?"
They were very
frightened.

They all swam to
the bottom of the lake.

The frogs hid there for a long time.

KEY WORDS

- **feel sorry for** (feel-felt-felt)
- **drop**
- **log**
- **go splash into the water** (go-went-gone)
- **frightened**
- **bottom**
- **hide** (hide-hid-hidden)
- **for a long time**
- **after a while**

- **see** (see-saw-seen)
- **do** (do-did-done)
- **nothing**
- **float around**
- **move**
- **climb out of**
- **call**
- **mind**

After a while, they saw that the log did
nothing.

It floated around.

It did not move much.

"Is this our new king?" they asked.

"He does not do much."

Some of the frogs climbed out of the water.

They sat on the log.

"Come on," they called to the others.

"We can sit on the king.

He does not mind."

After a while, the frogs got angry. 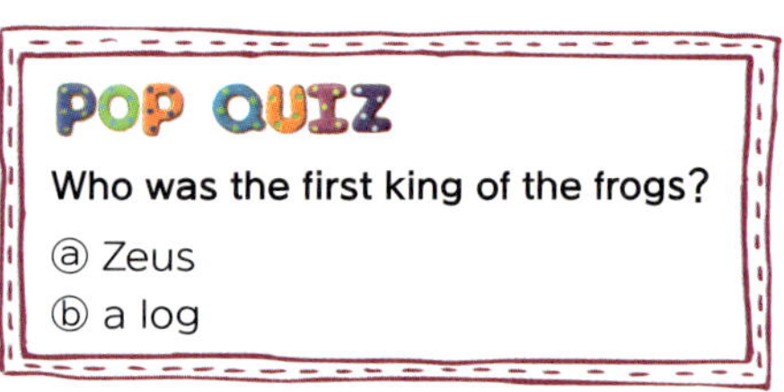

"This king is no good," they said.

"He does not do anything.

Give us a better king."

They croaked about it all day long.

So they went back to Zeus.

The frogs asked him for another king.

Zeus was a bit angry.

But he felt sorry for the frogs.

KEY WORDS

- **get angry** (get-got-gotten)
- **no good**
- **anything**
- **better**

- **go back**
- **another**
- **a bit**
- **eel**

- **wriggle**
- **the edge of**
- **stay**

So Zeus dropped an eel into the lake.

It wriggled about in the water.

"Help!" said the frogs.

"What is that?"

They were very frightened.

They all swam to the edge of the lake.

They stayed there for a long time.

After a while, they saw that the eel just swam
about.

It wriggled here and there.

It did not say much.

"Is this our new king?" asked the frogs.

"He is better than the old one."

So the frogs asked the eel, "What shall we do?"

"I don't mind," said the eel.

"Do what you like."

"What a good king!" said the frogs.

They swam around for a while.

They ate flies.

"Nothing has changed," they said at last.

"We want a better king."

They croaked about
it all day long.

So they went back to Zeus a third time. **Aha!**

"This king is no good," they said.

"He does not tell us anything.

Give us a better king."

Zeus was very angry with the frogs.

They croaked and complained all the time.

"I will send them a king," he said.

"They will not complain again."

KEY WORDS

- third
- tell (tell-told-told)
- complain
- all the time
- send (send-sent-sent)
- again

So Zeus sent a heron to the lake.

It had a long beak.

It had sharp eyes.

The heron stood at the edge of the water.

"Is this our new king?" said the frogs.

"He is watching us closely.

That is a good thing.

What a good king he is!"

But the heron was hungry.
He began to eat the frogs.
Each day, he ate a few more.
The lake grew quiet.
At last, there were
no frogs left to
croak upon
the lake.

▲ heron

- heron
- beak
- sharp
- **stand** (stand-stood-stood)
- **watch closely**

- **begin** (begin-began-begun)
- **each day**
- **a few more**
- **grow quiet** (grow-grew-grown)
- **leave** (leave-left-left)

Chapter One — Comprehension Quiz

A Who was the king of the frogs? Match the two sides.

❶ The first king •   • a) 

❷ The second king •   • b) 

❸ The third king •   • c) 

B Fill in each blank with the right word below.

swam	wriggled	dropped	climbed

❶ Zeus ______________ a log into the lake.

❷ The frogs ______________ to the bottom of the lake.

❸ The frogs ______________ out of the water onto the log.

❹ The eel ______________ about in the water.

❶ Why did Zeus give the frogs a king at the first time?

a) He felt pleased with them.

b) He felt sorry for them.

c) He felt angry with them.

d) He was very frightened.

❷ Why did the frogs think the heron was a good king?

a) It watched the frogs closely.

b) It had a long beak.

c) It stood at the edge of the water.

d) It was hungry.

❶ Who sat on the log? **Frogs / Zeus**

❷ Who dropped an eel into the lake? **Frogs / Zeus**

❸ Who complained all the time? **Frogs / Zeus**

❹ Who sent three different kings to the lake? **Frogs / Zeus**

Chapter Two

The Lion and the Mouse

Once, there was a mouse.

The mouse was very small.

It lived in the forest.

It lived in a small hole in a log.

The mouse liked to run about in the forest.

It liked the soft grass.

It liked the crisp leaves.

It ran about, looking for something to eat.

"Squeak, squeak," it said.

One day, the little mouse was running about
in the forest.
Suddenly, it could not run.
Something heavy was on its tail.
"Squeak, squeak," said the mouse.
"What is that on my tail?"

- once
- forest
- hole
- run about (run-ran-run)
- grass
- crisp
- leaf
- look for
- one day
- suddenly
- heavy
- tail

The mouse looked behind it.

There was a huge paw on its tail.

The paw belonged to a lion!

"*Growl, growl,*" said the lion.

"I am hungry.

I want to eat this little mouse."

"*Squeak, squeak.*

Please don't eat me," said the mouse.

"I am not very big.

If you eat me, you will still be hungry." Aha!

"But you will make a nice snack," said the lion.

He licked his lips.

KEY WORDS

- look behind
- paw
- belong to

- growl
- if
- still

- snack
- lick one's lips

The mouse tried to run away.

But the lion's paw was too heavy.

"*Squeak, squeak,*" said the mouse.

"If you let me go, I will help you."

The lion laughed.

"Help me?" he said.

"How could you

possibly help me?

I am so big.

You are so

small."

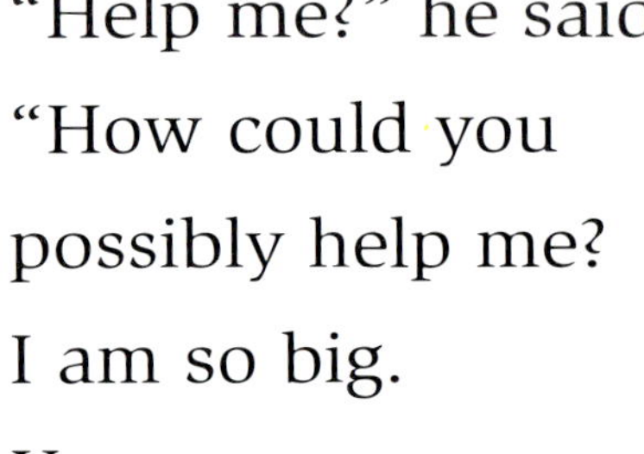

Choose the right description of the mouse.

ⓐ small and brave
ⓑ hungry and scared

- try to
- run away
- too
- let

- laugh
- possibly
- **know** (know-knew-known)
- brave

- **catch** (catch-caught-caught)

"I don't know," said the mouse.

"But one day, I will help you."

"*Growl, growl,*" said the lion.

"You are a brave mouse.

I will let you go.

But if I catch you again, I will eat you."

"*Squeak, squeak,*" said the mouse.

"Thank you so much."

It ran away into the forest.

It ran back to its hole in a log.

The lion lived at the edge of the forest.

He lay on a high rock where he could see everything.

The next morning, he woke up early.

It was still dark.

"*Growl, growl,*" said the lion.

"I am very hungry.

I will go hunting in the forest." **Aha!**

The lion stretched.

The lion yawned.

He jumped down from his rock.

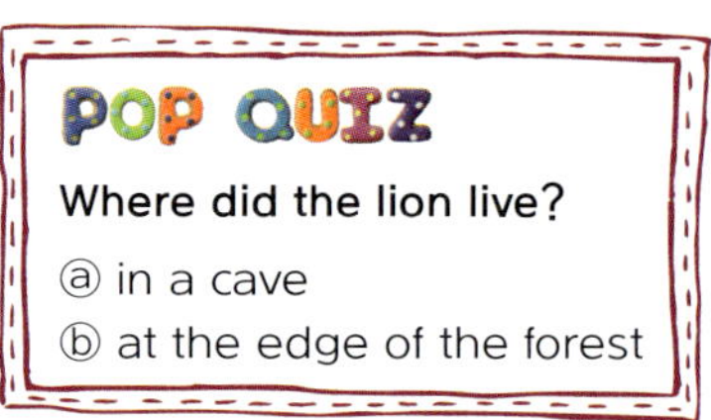

KEY WORDS

- **lie** (lie-lay-lain)
- **wake up** (wake-woke-woken)
- **early**
- **hunt**
- **stretch**
- **yawn**
- **jump down**

- **trap**
- **be made of** (make-made-made)
- **rope**
- **hold** (hold-held-held)
- **tightly**
- **roar**

He went into the forest.

But he walked into a trap!

The trap was made of ropes.

The ropes held the lion tightly.

"Roar, roar!" said the lion.

"I am trapped!"

The lion heard someone coming.

"*Roar, roar!*" said the lion.

"It is the hunter.

He is coming to get me."

The lion tried to escape.

He wriggled about.

But the ropes got tighter and tighter.

The hunter was coming with his gun.

Then, the lion heard another sound.

"Squeak, squeak. Squeak, squeak."

It was the little mouse!

The mouse jumped onto the lion's nose.

"Do you need help?" it said.

"I do need help," said the lion. Aha!

"I am trapped.

The hunter is coming

with his gun.

But you are so small.

How can you help

me?"

"Squeak, squeak," said the mouse.
"Watch and you will see."
There was a loud bang.
The hunter had arrived!
He was shooting birds in the trees.
"Help me, quickly!" said the lion.
The mouse jumped down from the lion's nose.

It ran down the lion's legs.

The ropes were tight and thick.

The mouse had sharp little teeth.

It began to nibble the ropes.

It nibbled and nibbled until the ropes fell off.

- loud
- bang
- arrive
- **shoot** (shoot-shot-shot)
- quickly
- thick
- teeth
- nibble
- until
- **fall off** (fall-fell-fallen)

The lion stood up.

He was free.

The mouse sat on his paw.

But the hunter had arrived.

He saw the lion.

He raised his gun.

"*Roar, roar!*" said the lion.

"You will not catch me."

The mouse was still sitting on the lion's paw.

The lion ran back to his rock.

The mouse held onto his fur.

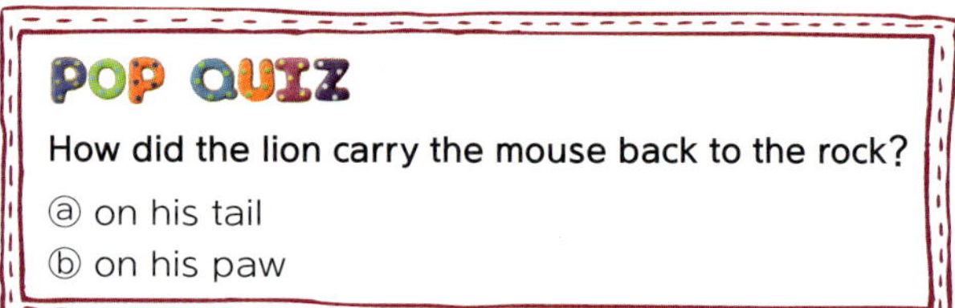

KEY WORDS

▪ free   ▪ raise   ▪ hold onto   ▪ fur

When he got there, he sat down.

He held the mouse in his paw.

"Thank you," said the lion.

"You kept your promise.

You helped me.

I will never try to eat you again."

"*Squeak, squeak,*" said the mouse.

"I may be small, but I can do big things." Aha!

"*Growl, growl,*" said the lion.

"I may be big, but I needed you today."

The lion and the mouse both lived in the forest.

They saw each other every day.

And the lion never tried to eat the mouse again.

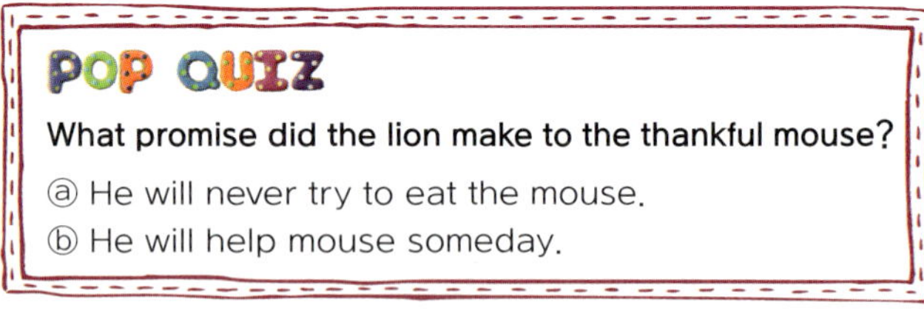

KEY WORDS

- sit down (sit-sat-sat)
- keep one's promise
  (keep-kept-kept)
- never
- may
- both
- each other
- every day

A Match each picture with all right words.

❶

❷

a) squeak, squeak

b) big

c) small

d) growl, growl

B Fill in each blank with the right word below.

soft	crisp	small	huge

❶ The mouse lived in a ______________ hole.

❷ There was ______________ grass in the forest.

❸ The mouse liked the ______________ leaves.

❹ There was a ______________ paw on the mouse's tail.

 Choose the best answer to each question.

❶ Which is true?

a) The mouse bit the lion.

b) The hunter shot the lion.

c) The lion and the mouse became friends.

d) The lion ate the mouse.

❷ Why did the mouse NOT move?

a) Its legs were tired.

b) The ground was icy.

c) It was caught in a trap.

d) A lion was holding its tail.

D Put the sentences in order.

❶ The lion went into the forest to hunt.

❷ The lion woke up.

❸ The lion walked into a trap.

❹ The lion jumped down from his rock.

__________ → __________ → __________ → __________

The Wolf in Sheep's Clothing

Once, there was a wolf.

He was a clever wolf.

But he was also very lazy.

He did not want to run fast.

He did not want to walk far.

He did not want to work hard.

The wolf loved to eat sheep.

It was not easy to catch a sheep.

The wolf had to run after them.

He had to climb up hills.

He had to jump over walls.

"There must be a better way to catch a sheep,"
said the wolf.

- sheep
- clothing
- clever
- lazy
- fast
- far
- work hard
- have to (have-had-had)
- run after
- climb up a hill
- jump over a wall
- must

Night fell.

The wolf hid at the edge of the forest.

He watched the shepherd and the sheep. 

The shepherd called the sheep together.

He put the sheep in a sheepfold.

The sheep were safe.

They had stone walls around them.

The shepherd shut the gate.

Then, he went away.

The wolf watched the sheep.

He saw their woolly fleeces.

Then, the wolf had an idea.

KEY WORDS

- fall
- shepherd
- call together
- put (put-put-put)
- sheepfold
- safe
- shut (shut-shut-shut)
- go away
- woolly
- fleece
- have an idea

"I shall dress up as a sheep," said the wolf.
"Then, the shepherd will put me in the sheepfold.
I shall eat as many sheep as I like. **Aha!**
I will not have to run after them."

- **dress up as**
- **next day**
- **find** (find-found-found)
- **put on**
- **look like**

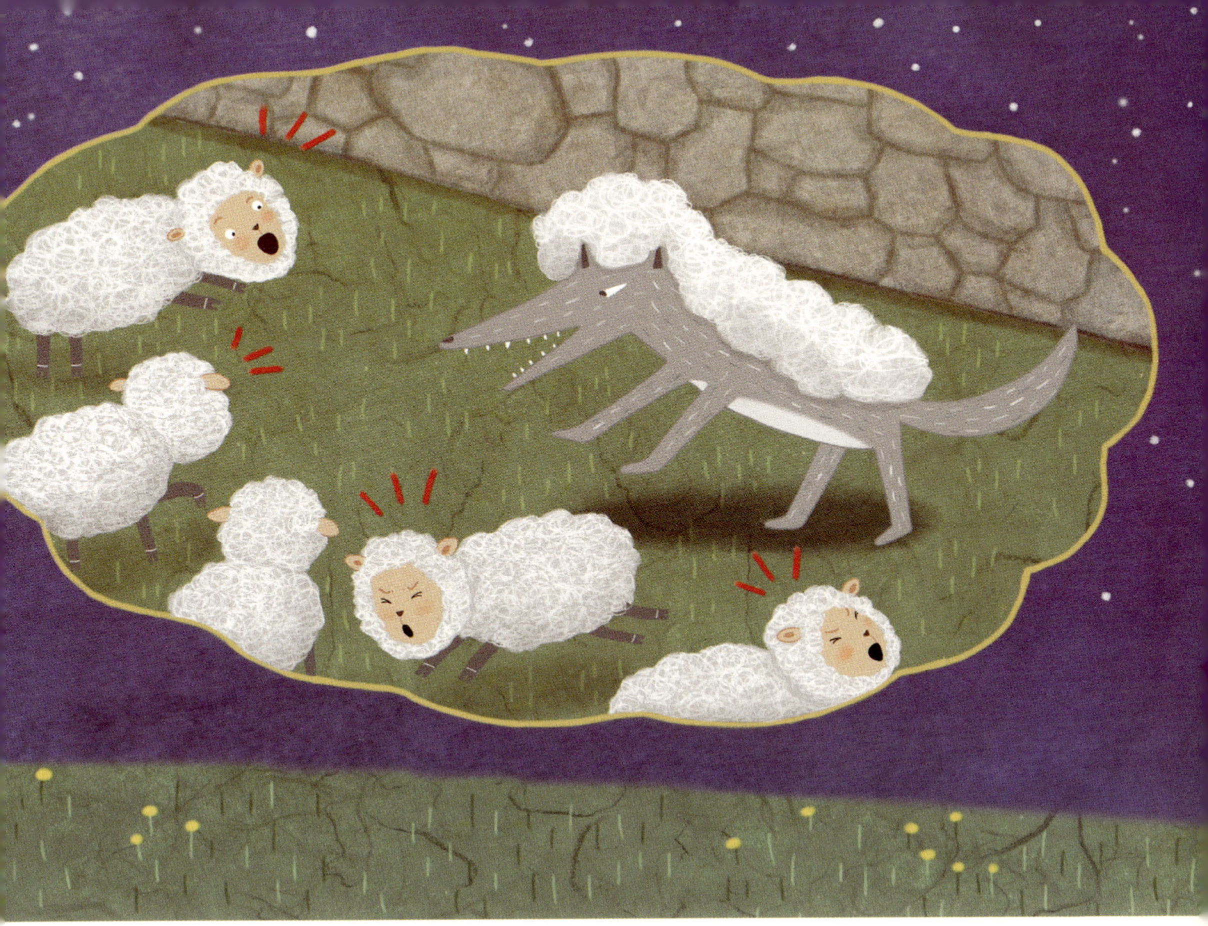

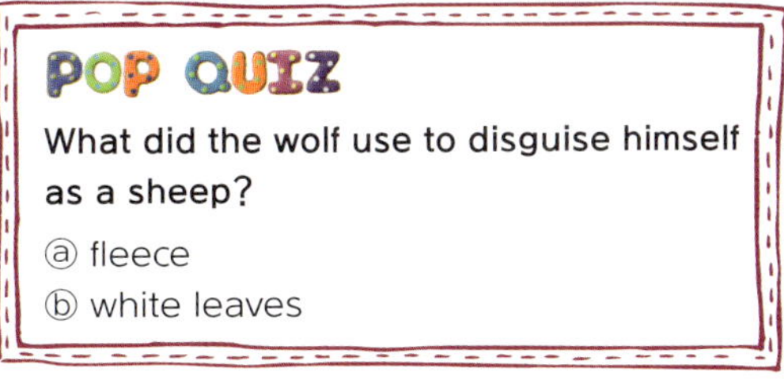

The next day, the wolf found a fleece.

He put it on his back.

He looked like a sheep.

POP QUIZ

What did the wolf use to disguise himself as a sheep?

ⓐ fleece

ⓑ white leaves

Night fell.

The wolf crept toward the sheep.

He went very slowly.

He went very quietly.

He did not want to scare the sheep.

The sheep looked up.

"Baa," they said.

"Baa, baa!" said the wolf.

The sheep went on eating. **Aha!**

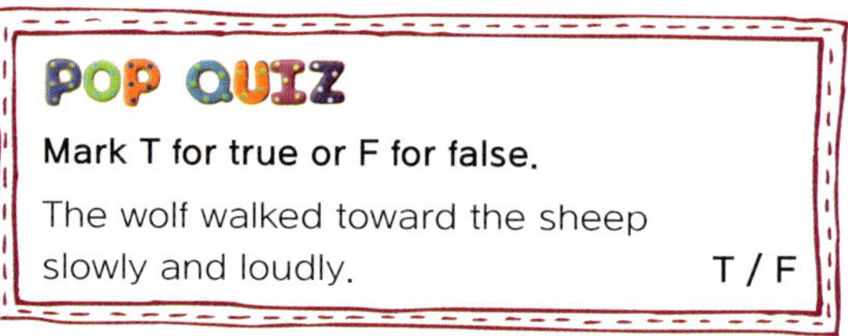

KEY WORDS

- **creep toward** (creep-crept-crept)
- **slowly**
- **quietly**
- **scare**
- look up
- baa
- plan
- work
- flock
- notice

"My plan has worked!" said the wolf.

"I look just like the other sheep."

The shepherd came to find his flock.

He did not notice the wolf.

The sheep went into the sheepfold.

The wolf went with them.

The shepherd went away.

"Now I shall have my meat!" said the wolf.

"I am so hungry.

Which sheep shall I have for my supper?"

He was ready to jump on the sheep.

But then he heard something.

There were footsteps.

Someone was whistling. **Aha!**

It was the shepherd!

He came back to the sheepfold.

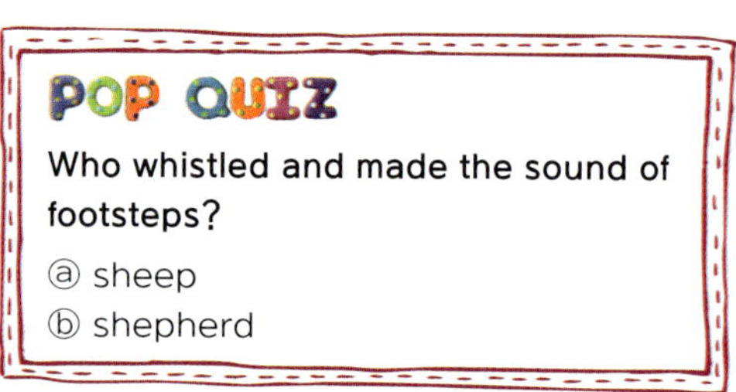

KEY WORDS

- meat
- supper
- be ready to
- jump on
- footstep

- whistle
- come back
- different
- beneath
- teach a lesson (teach-taught-taught)

The shepherd knew his sheep well.

He saw that one of them was different.

He saw some gray fur beneath the fleece.

"A wolf is in my flock!" he said.

"I will teach him a lesson."

So the shepherd said in a loud voice, "I am so hungry.

I will have meat for supper.

Which sheep shall I choose?"

The shepherd pulled out a long knife. 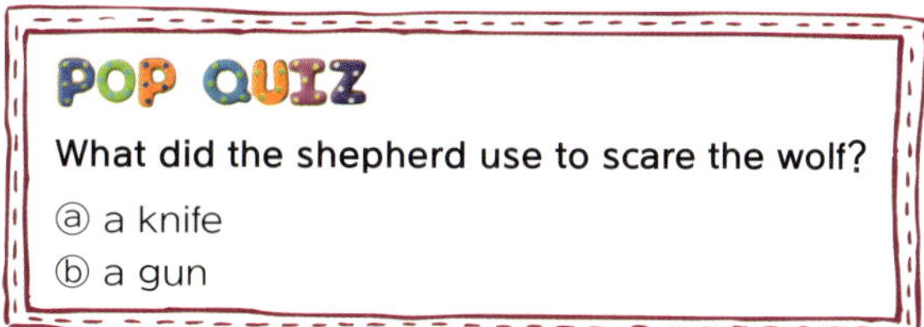

He opened the gate.

He came into the sheepfold.

The shepherd went to the wolf.

"This is a nice, fat sheep," said the shepherd.

"I shall have this one for my supper."

He lifted the knife.

> **POP QUIZ**
>
> What did the shepherd use to scare the wolf?
>
> ⓐ a knife
> ⓑ a gun

KEY WORDS

- voice
- **choose** (choose-chose-chosen)
- pull out
- lift

The wolf jumped up.

He ran out of the gate.

He ran away into the forest.

"I will never pretend to be a sheep again,"

said the wolf.

The shepherd laughed to himself.

"Don't worry," he said to the sheep. Aha!

"I will never eat you.

And the wolf has learned his lesson."

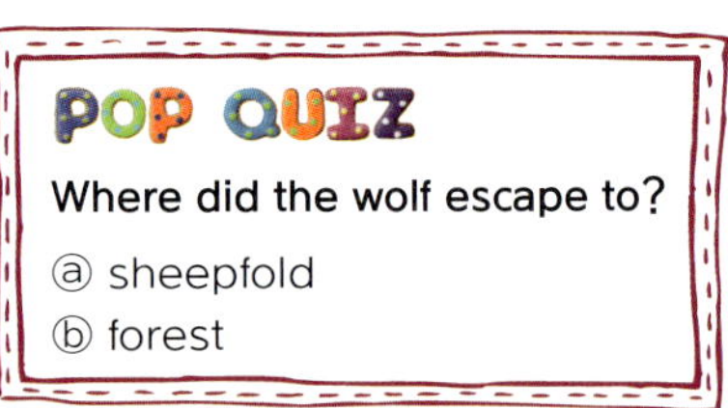

KEY WORDS

- jump up
- out of
- pretend
- laugh to oneself
- learn one's lesson

 **Chapter Three** # Comprehension Quiz

A Circle the right words to describe the wolf.

brave   lazy   stupid   clever   good

B Who said what? Match each line with the right character.

❶

❷

a) "I shall dress up as a sheep."

b) "I will teach him a lesson."

c) "This is a nice, fat sheep."

d) "My plan has worked!"

 Choose the best answer to each question.

❶ What did the wolf do to eat the sheep?

a) He dressed up as a shepherd.

b) He used a knife.

c) He pretended to be a sheep.

d) He whistled to the sheep.

❷ What is a group of sheep called?

a) a sheepfold

b) a flock

c) a fleece

d) a shepherd

D Mark T for true or F for false.

❶ The sheep were put in the sheepfold in the morning.　　T　F

❷ The sheep did not notice the wolf in the sheepfold.　　T　F

❸ The wolf ate a sheep for his supper.　　T　F

❹ The shepherd really wanted to eat one of his sheep.　　T　F

The Bundle of Sticks

Once, there was an old man.

He had three sons.

They argued all the time.

It was supper time.

The sons sat at the table.

They argued about who would have the
biggest share. **Aha!**

"I should have it.

I am the eldest," said the first son.

"I should have it.

I am the hungriest," said the second son.

"I should have it.

I am the thinnest," said the third son.

- a bundle of
- stick
- son
- argue

- biggest
- share
- should
- eldest

- hungriest
- thinnest

By the time they had finished arguing, the meal was cold.

Nobody ate it.

Their father shook his head.

"When would they learn to share together?"

After the meal, the sons went horse riding together.

"I should lead the way.

I am the eldest," said the first son.

"I should lead the way.

I am the cleverest," said the second son.

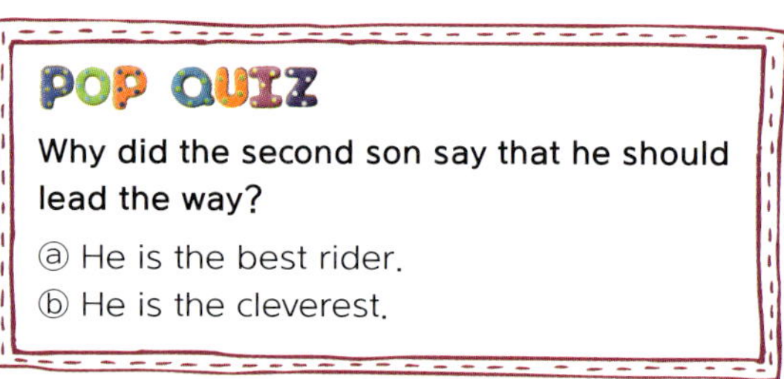

KEY WORDS

- by the time
- finish
- meal
- cold
- nobody
- **shake one's head** (shake-shook-shaken)

- go horse riding
- **lead the way** (lead-led-led)
- cleverest
- best
- rider
- get lost

"I should lead the way.

I am the best rider," said the third son.

They went different ways.

All three got lost.

They got home late.

Their father shook his head.

"When would they learn to work together?"

The next morning, the father fell ill.

The sons stood around his bed.

"I think I am going to die," said their father.

"I must tell you something important."

"Tell me. I am the eldest," said the first son.

"Tell me. I am the best at listening," said the second son.

"Tell me. I have the best memory," said the third son.

They talked and talked.

Nobody listened to the father.

He shook his head.

"When would they learn to listen together?"

The father called his servant.

"Fetch a bundle of sticks," he said.

The servant brought the sticks.

They were tied together with rope.

"Stop arguing!" said the father to his sons. [Aha!]

The sons did not hear him.

"I said, stop arguing!"

The father began to cough.

He coughed and coughed.

"I am going to die.

Listen to what I say."

The sons stopped arguing.

KEY WORDS

- servant
- fetch
- **bring** (bring-brought-brought)

- tie (↔ untie)
- cough

They listened to their father.
He called the first son.
"Break that bundle of
sticks."
The first son smiled.
"I can do that,"
he said.
"It will be easy."
The first son tried to
break the sticks. 
He tried and tried with
all his strength.
But he could not break the
bundle of sticks.

The father called the second son.

"Break that bundle of sticks."

The second son smiled.

"I can do that," he said.

"It will be easy."

The second son tried to break the sticks.

He tried and tried with all his strength.

But he could not break the bundle of sticks.

POP QUIZ

What did the father ask his sons to do?

ⓐ to carry the bundle of sticks

ⓑ to break the bundle of sticks

The father called the third son.

"Break that bundle of sticks."

The third son smiled.

"I can do that," he said.

"It will be easy."

The third son tried
to break the sticks.

He tried and tried
with all his strength.

But he could not break
the bundle of sticks.

The father smiled.

He told the servant to untie the rope. Aha!

"Each of you take a stick," said the father.

"Break it in two."

Each of the sons took a stick.

Each of them broke his stick in two.

"It's so easy," they said.

One by one, they broke the sticks.

They helped each other.

It was easy when they worked together.

Chapter Four

Comprehension Quiz

A Who said what? Match each line with the right person.

❶ 
first son

❷ 
second son

❸ 
third son

a) "I am the eldest."

b) "I am the best rider."

c) "I am the hungriest."

B Circle the right word for each underlined part.

❶ "I am the thinnest," said the (three / third) son.

❷ When (wood / would) they learn to share?

❸ The father (called / cold) his servant.

❹ Each of them broke his stick in (two / too).

C Choose the best answer to each question.

❶ Why did nobody eat the meal?

a) It did not taste good.

b) It was cold.

c) Nobody was hungry.

d) Everyone was working.

❷ What did the sons do after supper?

a) They collected some sticks.

b) They went to bed.

c) They talked to their father.

d) They went horse riding.

D Put the sentences in order.

❶ The sons tried to break the sticks.

❷ The sons sat at the table for supper.

❸ The sons stood around their father's bed.

❹ The sons went horse riding.

________ → ________ → ________ → ________

Let's Review the Story

Fill in the blanks to review the story.

Title: Aesop's Fables

Story 1
- **Title:** The Frogs Ask for a King
- **Main Characters:** some frogs, Zeus

1. The frogs ask Zeus to give them a __________.
2. Zeus gives them a __________, and an eel. The frogs still complain.
3. Zeus gives them a __________. It eats all of the frogs.

Story 2
- **Title:** The Lion and the __________
- **Main Characters:** a lion, a mouse

1. The __________ catches the mouse. The mouse promises to help the lion one day.
2. The lion is caught in a __________. The mouse helps the lion to get out of it.

Story 3
- **Title:** The __________ in Sheep's Clothing
- **Main Characters:** a wolf, a shepherd

1. The lazy wolf dresses up as a __________ to catch a sheep.
2. The __________ sees the wolf in the sheepfold and he says he will eat the wolf.
3. The wolf runs away.

Story 4
- **Title:** The Bundle of Sticks
- **Main Characters:** a father, three __________

1. The three sons always __________.
2. The father gives the sons a bundle of __________. He asks them to __________ the sticks.
3. They can only break the sticks by helping each other.

Let's Think & Talk

Think about the following questions and answer them freely.

❶ Why did Zeus send a heron as the third king to the frogs? Think about the reason and explain it.

❷ If you were the mouse that had been caught by a lion, would you be able to get away? Tell us how you would get away.

❸ Have you ever been in big trouble because of cunning behavior like the wolf's? If you have, tell us in detail.

❹ If you were the three brothers' father, how would you make them reconcile?

Let's Review the Story

Title: Aesop's Fables

Story 1
- **Title**: The Frogs Ask for a King
- **Main Characters**: some frogs, Zeus

1. The frogs ask Zeus to give them a **king** .
2. Zeus gives them a **log** , and an eel. The frogs still complain.
3. Zeus gives them a **heron** . It eats all of the frogs.

Story 2
- **Title**: The Lion and the **Mouse**
- **Main Characters**: a lion, a mouse

1. The **lion** catches the mouse. The mouse promises to help the lion one day.
2. The lion is caught in a **trap** . The mouse helps the lion to get out of it.

Story 3
- **Title**: The **Wolf** in Sheep's Clothing
- **Main Characters**: a wolf, a shepherd

1. The lazy wolf dresses up as a **sheep** to catch a sheep.
2. The **shepherd** sees the wolf in the sheepfold and he says he will eat the wolf.
3. The wolf runs away.

Story 4
- **Title**: The Bundle of Sticks
- **Main Characters**: a father, three **sons**

1. The three sons always **argue** .
2. The father gives the sons a bundle of **sticks** . He asks them to **break** the sticks.
3. They can only break the sticks by helping each other.

- Aesop's Fables
- Level 1
- 18 Questions

  (Vocabulary 5 / Reading Comprehension 10 /

  Sentence Structure & Grammar 3)

1. Which of the following is similar to the word "huge"?
   ① cold   ② warm
   ③ big   ④ small

2. Which of these words means "escape"?

   > The lion tried to escape.

   ① roar   ② growl
   ③ move   ④ get away

3. Which of the following pair has the wrong past tense form of the listed verb?
   ① shut − shut
   ② find − found
   ③ choose − chose
   ④ pull − pull

4. Choose the right word for the blank.

   > "Fetch a bundle __________ sticks," he said.

   ① on   ② to
   ③ of   ④ for

5. Which of the following is pronounced differently compared to the others?
   ① knife   ② king
   ③ knee   ④ know

6. Why did the frogs NOT like the log?
    ① It was rough to sit on.
    ② It was unkind to them.
    ③ It didn't do much.
    ④ It told them what to do.

7. Why did the lake which the frogs lived in grow quiet?
    ① The eel had gone.
    ② The frogs stopped croaking.
    ③ The heron ate all of the frogs.
    ④ There were no flies left.

8. Who sent the king to the frogs?
    ① the log
    ② Zeus
    ③ the eel
    ④ the heron

9. In "The Lion and the Mouse", where did the mouse live?
    ① on a rock
    ② at the top of a tree
    ③ in a log
    ④ in the grass

10. Who set up the trap?
    ① the other lion
    ② the mouse
    ③ the hunter
    ④ the birds

11. Choose one thing that the wolf doesn't need to do to catch a sheep.

    ① running after the sheep
    ② climbing up hills
    ③ swimming across rivers
    ④ jumping over walls

12. Where do the sheep sleep every night?

    ① in the forest
    ② around the lake
    ③ in the sheepfold
    ④ in a farm

13. Why did the wolf go slowly and quietly toward the sheep?

    ① He did not want to scare them.
    ② He had sore feet.
    ③ He was tired.
    ④ He did not want to wake them up.

14. Why did the three brothers' father want his sons to stop arguing?

    ① He wanted they would eat their supper.
    ② He wanted they would not get lost.
    ③ He wanted he would get well again.
    ④ He wanted they would learn to work together.

15. How did the sons break the bundle of sticks?

    ① They broke them one at a time.
    ② They used a hammer.
    ③ They asked the servant to break them.
    ④ They tied a rope around them.

16.

> The <u>sheep</u> <u>went</u> <u>on</u> to <u>eat</u>.
> ① ② ③ ④

17.

> <u>But</u> you <u>will</u> <u>made</u> a nice <u>snack</u>.
> ① ② ③ ④

18. Choose the correct word for the blank.

> I am the _______.

① thin ② best thin

③ thinnest ④ most thin

Sarah J. Dodd
Sarah J. Dodd is an experienced primary school teacher who resides in the UK, but has also lived and taught in Australia. She has a PhD in Science and a certificate in Creative Writing. She has published several books for children: "An Angel Anyway" (Anyway Press, 2008) the "Little Angels" series (Lion Children's Books, 2009/10), "The Lion Picture Bible" (Lion Children's Books, 2015) and "Legs: the tale of a meerkat lost and found" (Lion Children's Books, 2015). Her poetry for children has also been highly commended and published in the anthology "Let in the Stars" (Manchester Metropolitan University, 2014).
She is currently working on further picture books for the very young, and a novel for older children.

Aesop's Fables

Written by Aesop
Retold by Sarah J. Dodd
Illustrated by Dukjin Lee

First published December 2014
3rd printing July 2023

Publisher: Kyudo Chung
Editors: Juyon Choi, Jiyeong Park, Kyunghee Jang
Designers: Eunhee Lee, Elim

Published and distributed by
Happy House, an imprint of DARAKWON, Inc.
Darakwon Bldg., 211 Munbal-ro, Paju-si, Gyeonggi-do, 10881, Republic of Korea
Tel: 82-2-736-2031(ext. 250)   Fax: 82-2-732-2037
Homepage: www.ihappyhouse.co.kr

ISBN: 978-89-6653-158-5 18740 / 978-89-6653-156-1 18740(set)

[Components]
• Audio Files & Answer Keys & Korean Translation: Free download at
www.ihappyhouse.co.kr

 This book is made with nontoxic materials.